Reinh

The Holy Spirit Baptism

The Holy Spirit Baptism
English

ISBN 3-935057-12-1

Edition 6, Printing 1
10,000 copies

Originally published by CfaN 1992
ISBN 3-9802990-0-7

1,780,000 copies in print
in 30 languages

Cover design by Isabelle Brasche
Cover photographs by Tom Henschke
Typeset by David Lant

Published by Full Flame GmbH,
Postfach 60 05 95, 60335 Frankfurt am Main,
Germany.
www.fullflame.com

Visit the CfaN web site at www.cfan.org

Printed in China

Part One

THE HOLY SPIRIT BAPTISM: WHAT IT IS

THE EDICT

The most wonderful sound ever heard was about to fall on the ears of the tens of thousands of people gathered in the Temple courts at Jerusalem. The final rituals of a national festival were taking place. All eyes followed a golden pitcher filled with water and wine. A drink offering was ready to be poured out to the Lord.

A priest lifted the gleaming vessel in the sunshine and paused. Silence fell as the people strained to hear the sacred water splashing into a bronze bowl at the altar.

Then came the interruption: a voice not known for a thousand years. A voice that made the spine tingle. It was the voice of Jesus Christ, the Son of God. He was the Word who had spoken in the beginning and called forth heaven and earth into existence. Now at Jerusalem He stood and issued a royal and divine edict, changing the dispensation of God:

> *"If anyone thirsts, let him come to Me and drink. He who believes in Me, as the Scripture has said, out of his heart will flow rivers of living water."* (John 7:37-38, NKJ)

STREAMS IN THE DESERT

"Rivers of living water"! Not bottles, but rivers – fresh, lively, sparkling, abundant, unending.

Some people live for what comes out of a bottle. The world's supermarkets have very little that is fresh. Pre-packed pleasure is big business, with canned music, films, records, books. Television provides the highlights of life for millions of people, just watching others live or pretending to live, even for children, who forget how to play.

People are always "going to" live ... after things change, after working hours, when they have money, when they get married, retire or go on holiday. Jesus came to give us life NOW. NO WAITING, wherever we are, whatever we are doing. He makes life live.

Jesus came to give us life NOW. NO WAITING, wherever we are, whatever we are doing. He makes life live.

God wrote His plan for Israel in the wilderness across a blackboard 40 years wide. The Israelites did not have to drink stale, flat water from skins. The Lord opened bubbling streams from a rock (Exodus 17:1-7). The Temple drink offering was a celebration in memory of that wilderness water (Numbers 20:1-13). Jesus, however, gave it a new and glorious meaning, a symbol of the outpouring of the Holy Spirit.

ONLY JESUS

THIS JESUS! Nobody else had ever dared make such an amazing claim – and fulfill it. He would ascend to glory where Creation began and change the order of things. Something not known before would surge from heaven to earth. He called it *"the promise of the Father"* (Acts 1:4, KJV). **THE** promise. Out of over 8,000 promises in God's Word, the designation of THE promise makes it stand singularly and significantly alone. Christ made it His own promise. The Father's gift to Him is His gift to us, as John the Baptist said:

> *"I myself did not know him; but he who sent me to baptize with water said to me, 'He on whom you see the Spirit descend and remain, this is he who baptizes with the Holy Spirit.' And I have seen and have borne witness that this is the Son of God." (John 1:33-34, RSV)*

WHEN WORDS FAIL

John used a different expression here instead of *"rivers of living water."* Scripture has many other terms, such as:

Being baptized in holy fire (Matthew 3:11, Luke 3:16); *"endued with power"* (Luke 24:49, NKJ); anointed with the oil of God; immersed in the Spirit; *"filled with the Spirit"* (Ephesians 5:18, NIV). Walking, praying, living in the Spirit (Galatians 5:25, Romans 8:26, KJV). Our bodies being temples of the Holy Spirit (1 Corinthians 6:19, NIV). Having *"another Comforter"* besides Christ Himself (John 14:16 KJV).

These are sketches, but color and details have to be added. The Bible is a picture gallery of the Holy Spirit in operation; it portrays signs, wonders and miracles. Men looking as if "they had been with Jesus." The world turned upside down. People coming to "know the Lord," enjoying a new experience. Not just religious enthusiasts, churchgoers, but a new breed with vibrant faith. Paul says that God *"... made us alive with Christ even when we were dead in transgressions ... "* (Ephesians 2:5, NIV) and that we are *"... strengthened with all power according to his glorious might"* (Colosians 1:11, NIV). The Lord Jesus Christ Himself promised it: *"'But you will receive power when the Holy Spirit comes on you'"* (Acts 1:8, NIV).

We as born-again believers are special; we are saints, and the baptism in the Spirit is Christ's next major experience for us. Jesus alone made it possible when He died and rose and sat down at the right hand of the Majesty on High. What a gift!

WHO IS THE HOLY SPIRIT?

The Lord does not send publicity by heavenly mail to tell us who He is. The works performed by His Spirit are seen on earth. **The Holy Spirit is a Person; He is God in action.** Creation came as *"the Spirit of God was hovering over the waters"* (Genesis 1:2, NIV). Then, when God chose His servants, the power of the Holy Spirit rested upon them:

> *"The Lord has chosen Bezalel ... and he has filled him with the Spirit of God, with skill, ability and knowledge. ... And he has given both*

him and Oholiab ... the ability to teach others." (Exodus 35:30, 31, 34, NIV)

"The spirit of the Lord came upon him [Othniel], *and he judged Israel."* (Judges 3:10, KJV)

The Spirit *"clothed Gideon with Himself,"* (Judges 6:34, AMP) and Gideon defended Israel (Judges 6:11-8:35). The Spirit moved Samson to acts of supernormal strength (Judges 13:1-16:31). The Spirit of the Lord came upon Jephtha and delivered Israel's foes into his hands (Judges 11:1-12:7).

After these judges the prophet Samuel guided an entire nation for a life-time. How? *"Holy men of God spake (as they were) moved by the Holy Ghost"* (2 Peter 1:21). The prophet Micah testified, *"I am full of power by the spirit of the Lord"* (Micah 3:8, KJV).

This is that Spirit whom Christ promised: the Spirit of wisdom and knowledge; creative, empowering, healing; the Spirit of strength, confidence and virtue.

These are portraits of the Holy Spirit. This is that Spirit whom Christ promised: the Spirit of wisdom and knowledge; creative, empowering, healing; the Spirit of strength, confidence and virtue.

God's power is not a kind of supercharge for people already gifted with great personality and drive, but is for those who need it, the weak and the unknown. *"He gives power to the faint, and to him who has no might he increases strength"* (Isaiah 40:29, RSV).

FOUR GREAT PICTURES

Four of the pictures in the Bible gallery should be examined carefully.

The first picture: Moses put his hands on 70 elders at the Tent of Meeting, and the Spirit of God came upon them. At that moment back in the camp, Eldad and Medad were also endued and began to prophesy. A young man ran to tell Moses. Joshua thought Moses should have a monopoly on prophesying and urged, *"'Moses, my lord, stop them!'"* Far from objecting, Moses said, *"'Are you jealous for my sake? I wish that all the Lord's people were prophets and that the Lord would put His Spirit on them!'"* (Numbers 11:24-29, NIV)

Seventy at once! That was the most for over 1200 years. The experience was rare, usually temporary and only for individuals. However, Moses' wish lay in many hearts while long centuries passed.

The second picture: The Temple Solomon had built was in full operation, but sin had weakened the nation. A prophet stood in Jerusalem, bringing a warning of judgment. Through the telescope of prophecy Joel had seen distant skies black with war clouds, terror and destruction, Israel laid waste – which, as we now know, proved Joel a true prophet. However, Joel was telling Israel more. Beyond the gathering storm, he saw bright skies, not merely recovery, but a wonderful New Thing.

"And afterward, I will pour out my Spirit upon all people. Your sons and daughters will prophesy, your old men will dream dreams, your young men will see visions. Even on my servants, both men and women, I will pour out my Spirit in those days. I will show wonders in the heavens and on the earth, blood and fire and billows of smoke." (Joel 2:28-30, NIV)

In those days young slave girls poured water on the hands of their mistresses to wash them, but God promised to pour out His Spirit even on them. In fact, it meant that the HOLY SPIRIT WOULD BE POURED OUT WORLDWIDE UPON ALL MANNER OF PEOPLE.

This was sensational. What He had once granted to only a handful of His chosen servants would be a privilege everyone could call his own. It was too hard for many to imagine or believe. But God said it, and His Word stands forever.

The third picture: John the Baptist in leather clothing stood on the bank of the Jordan River. He was the first prophet of God in 400 years. Crowds came out to hear him and be baptized. His thunderous message called on Israel to repent and prepare because the long-awaited Coming One would appear.

The Holy Spirit would he poured out worldwide upon all manner of people.

"I baptize you with water for repentance. But after me will come one who is more powerful than I, whose sandals I am not fit to carry. He

will baptize you with the Holy Spirit and with fire." (Matthew 3:11, NIV)

Twenty-four hours later, among the candidates for baptism, John saw a young man wading through the waters and stood aghast: "YOU! JESUS! I am not worthy to baptize you. You should baptize me!" God had shown John that Jesus was that promised *"'one who was to come'"* (Matthew 11:3, Luke 7:19, 20, NIV). He would perform a rite far greater than John in the Jordan. Jesus the Baptist would not use a physical element, water, but heavenly fire, which is a spiritual element. John stood in the cold waters of the Jordan, but Jesus stood in a river of liquid fire. John had baptized for a few short days; Jesus would baptize down through the ages, not just one group on the day of Pentecost, but *"all flesh."* He is doing so even now, some 700,000 days later!

The fourth picture: Fearing the authorities who had executed Jesus, 120 disciples came together quietly. Jesus had said, *"'Stay in the city* [Jerusalem] *until you have been clothed with power from on high'"* (Luke 24:49, NIV). They sat and waited, and the world forgot them. Nothing happened; no marvels occurred; everything seemed so ordinary.

The tenth day was a Sunday, the Feast of Weeks, also called Pentecost. At nine in the morning, a Temple priest lifted the bread of the firstfruits and waved it before the Lord. As if this were a signal for the ascended Christ, a divine tornado tore through the skies above Jerusalem.

Jesus Himself had broken through the heavens in His shattering and victorious **Ascension**. Now through the opened skies there was a **Descension.** The Holy Spirit came, demonstrating that the way into the heavenlies was open. Praise God, it has never been closed since! When the curtain of the Temple was ripped as Jesus died, the priests probably tried to stitch it together again. Nobody can stitch up this rent in the heavens, not even the devil and all his minions. It is a new and living way, open forever.

Moses saw God as fire in the bush. Now through this door of glory, which no man could shut, the same fire, the Holy Spirit, came. Amber flames settled in burning beauty upon the head of each waiting disciple. Glory that filled all heaven now crowded into the breasts of those present. The Holy Spirit was in them and on them. Men had never experienced it before. There were no words to describe it. This was unutterable. Then God gave them words, new tongues and languages to tell *"the wonderful works of God"* (Acts 2:11, KJV) like inspired psalmists.

Moses saw God as fire in the bush. Now through this door of glory, which no man could shut, the same fire, the Holy Spirit, came.

THE BAPTISM AND OTHER WORKINGS

We receive salvation and are born again through the Holy Spirit. But that is not the end of His work. His activities are manifold. He empowers us for witnessing in particular. The baptism in the Spirit means that people saved by grace and born again can have new experiences and become Spirit-energized witnesses for Christ.

How necessary this is! It was vital even for the disciples who had healed the sick and cast out demons. That was possible only as long as Christ was by their sides. The Lord Jesus told them to wait until they were endued with the Spirit before they went forth into the fields for service. Mary the mother of Christ was one example. She had certainly known the Holy Spirit in her life to bring about the birth of Jesus, but she too waited at Jerusalem for this further work of the Spirit, called *"the promise of the Father"* (Acts 1:4, KJV). If she needed it, we all do.

The baptism in the Spirit means that people saved by grace and born again can have new experiences and become Spirit-energized witnesses for Christ.

The explanation is simple: The disciples belonged to Christ. He said so, and as long as He was with them on earth, they could do marvelous works. Then He ascended to God, and they felt lonely and frightened. However, the Lord had made a promise: He would send *"another Comforter,"* that is, the Holy Spirit (John 14:16, KJV).

The word "comforter" suggests "someone walking by your side." Jesus had walked by their sides for over three years, and He was their first great Comforter. Then that other Person, *"another Comforter,"* the Holy Spirit, came on the Day of Pentecost. It was like having Jesus with them again, and they were able to carry out the Great Commission to preach the Gospel, heal the sick, cast out devils and work wonders as before, in short, the work of witnessing, which is the privilege and responsibility of every born-again person (Matthew 28:19-20, Mark 16:15-18).

First, we must come to Christ and give ourselves to Him, and then receive the power baptism. Our very lives should be evidence of His Resurrection.

The same situation exists for us. First, we must come to Christ and give ourselves to Him, and then receive the power baptism. Our very lives should be evidence of His Resurrection. It is more than talk that is needed – It is people manifesting the fullness of the Spirit.

The word "baptism" did not have a religious meaning originally. It is from the trade of dyeing fabrics. The English equivalent is "dipping." The cloth or garment is dipped into the dye, and the cloth takes on the color or character of the dye. When Christ baptizes us in the Spirit, we partake of the "color" or character of the Spirit, *"partakers of the divine nature"* (2 Peter 1:4, KJV). The Spirit is in us, and we in the Spirit; we are people of the Holy Spirit.

It was not just seeing Jesus or hearing His voice which made the disciples the great people they were, because *"some believed and some doubted,"* (Matthew 28:17; cf. Mark 16:13, 14 and Luke 24:41) but the Holy Spirit baptism. They shut the door when they met for fear of the Jews (John 20:19). They certainly did not shout in the streets, "Jesus is alive!" They met secretly, at first away in Galilee, and they even went fishing (John 21:3). All that changed, however, on the Day of Pentecost. Instead of their being afraid of the Jewish crowds, the crowds trembled before them and cried out, *"'Brothers, what shall we do?'"* (Acts 2:37, NIV) This was as Jesus said:

> *"But you will receive power when the Holy Spirit comes on you; and you will be my witnesses ... to the ends of the earth."* (Acts 1:8, NIV)

HOW IT FIRST HAPPENED

Now we look again at the fourth picture:

> *When the day of Pentecost had come, they were all together in one place. And suddenly a sound came from heaven like the rush of a mighty wind, and it filled all the house where they were sitting. And there appeared to them tongues as of fire, distributed and resting on each one of them. And they were all filled with the Holy Spirit and began to speak in other tongues, as the Spirit gave them utterance.* (Acts 2:1-4, RSV)

What divine power and glory! This second chapter of Acts is noisy and action-packed. The heavenly Father does not make empty promises, just to build up our hopes and then laugh at us. Christ had said, *"Go into all the world ..."* (Mark 16:15, NIV). The moment those "tongues of fire" touched their heads, it put the "go" into them. God acted and then they acted. Divine action caused human reaction, which is why this book is called the Acts of the Apostles.

There was an inflow from heaven, and there had to be an outflow. *"Out of his heart will flow rivers ...."* (John 7:38, NKJ), not just "into." It was not for emotional satisfaction. The disciples did not say, "Let us have a prayer meeting for power like this every week." They never again asked for power for themselves, because they knew that they had it already. The apostle Peter said to the cripple at the Gate Beautiful, *"'What I do have I give to you'"* (Acts 3:6, NIV, emphasis added).

The Trinity, the whole Godhead, set the plans of salvation and evangelism into motion.

Nor did they just sit, appointing a chairman and passing resolutions on social problems. They could not contain themselves! They had to be up and doing. Peter stood, electrified. And ... the Christian age began; the world heard the first Gospel sermon.

The result? Three thousand people received salvation. That was the reason for Pentecost. In fact, the Trinity, the whole Godhead, set the plans of salvation and evangelism into motion. The Father joined with the ascended Lord to send the Spirit to save a lost world (Isaiah 48:16). That is the main purpose of the baptism in the Spirit. That is what God is doing: saving people. What are we doing? This baptism is not for thrills, but to help us work alongside the Lord. We know why Jesus and the Holy Spirit came. Why are WE here?

What a day Pentecost was! "Rivers" flowed that eventually flooded the Roman Empire. People sigh and wish they were back in the days of the early Church, but it was neither the days nor the men which made the time special. It was the baptism in the Holy Spirit. Without it, the disciples would probably have gone back to being fishermen in Galilee and grown old telling tales of strange events when they were young. Instead, they changed the world.

That baptism is for all today.

FOR TODAY

Some people want to deprive believers today, saying the baptism in the Spirit with signs following was only for the first believers, "until the Church got under way"; they suggest that we have to manage without the miraculous gifts of those believers. That would make the early Christians an elite group, as if we could not be Christians in the way they were. However, not a word in the Bible suggests such a thing. It is a theory invented by unbelief. In fact, when Paul went to Ephesus twenty years after the Church had been well planted, twelve people were baptized in the Spirit (Acts 19:6-7).

Every generation needs Pentecost. In A.D. 30 the world population was one hundred million. Today it is six billion and growing rapidly. Ten times more people today than in the first century do not know about Jesus. The Church still needs planting. Unbelief and complete ignorance of God exist everywhere. Surely our need for the power of the Holy Spirit is far more desperate.

Therefore, I want to explain to you carefully, from the Bible itself, why and how that same baptism is for us today. Read what Peter preached to the multitude on the Day of Pentecost, under the anointing of the Spirit, when he explained who could be baptized in the Holy Spirit:

> *"For the promise is to you and to your children and to all that are far off, every one whom the Lord our God calls to him."* (Acts 2:39, RSV)

First, Peter said it is *"'to you,'"* the very people he had just accused saying, *"Ye have taken* [Jesus], *and by wicked hands have crucified and slain* [him]*."* (Acts 2:23, KJV). Yet he announced, *"'Repent, and be baptized every one of you in the name of Jesus Christ for the forgiveness of your sins; and you shall receive the gift of the Holy Spirit'"* (Acts 2:38, RSV). These were the same people that Jesus had called *"an evil generation,"* (Luke 11:29, KJV) *"faithless and perverse"* (Matthew 17:17, Luke 9:41, KJV).

Second, he said it is *"'to your children,'"* the next generation. Some people would not become parents until later. It could be that 100 years after the Day of Pentecost people would receive this blessing and speak in tongues. One woman mentioned in Luke 2:36 had been a widow for 84 years. However, the word "children" referred not only to their families, but also to their descendants, that is, the children of Israel.

Third, Peter said, *"'to all that are far off,'"* i.e., in time and distance, at the ends of the earth where Christ had commissioned the Church to take the Gospel (Matthew 28:19-20, Mark 16:15-16). This would take many years, far beyond the apostolic age. New Zealand, for example, would be one of the ends of the earth; no missionary arrived there until 1814. Indeed, the task is not completed even today; therefore, we still need that same power.

Fourth, Peter hammered it home, *"'every one whom the Lord our God calls to him.'"* Those "God calls" are those who come to Christ. *"'No one can come to me unless the Father who sent me draws him'"* (John 6:44, NIV). All believers are called and are promised the same gift of the Holy Spirit that Peter and his 119 friends had just received. Do what the disciples did, and you will get what the disciples got. Believe God's promises given to us all, *"And be not drunk with wine ..., but be filled with the Spirit"* (Ephesians 5:18, KJV).

Only Jesus is the Baptizer, nobody else. Do not settle for a secondhand experience. Have your own Pentecost.

Only Jesus is the Baptizer, nobody else. Do not settle for a secondhand experience. Have your own Pentecost. Do not try to cash in on someone else's experience in a charismatic meeting. The fire of the Holy Spirit did not arrive in one big, general flame so that all could gather and warm themselves, conducting cozy conferences.

Rather, it came in separate *"tongues,"* little flames that *"sat upon each of them"* (Acts 2:3, KJV). This was very significant: Those tongues of fire were in fact potent and portable power stations which would move with the people wherever they went.

We live in a spiritually dark and cold world. The best way not to freeze is to be aglow with the Holy Spirit. God will light a fire on the altar of your own heart so that you can be a fire-lighter. Warm others, do not depend on others to warm you!

Part Two

THE HOLY SPIRIT BAPTISM: HOW TO RECEIVE IT

BELIEVING THE GIVER

Thousands of people come into our campaign meetings as unbelievers. Some of them are really far away from God: wicked, immoral, addicted, bound by the occult or working hard for religions that do nothing for them. They must first receive salvation. Paul said to converts in his day, *"You were washed clean"* (1 Corinthians 6:11, AMP). Perhaps unclean spirits had previously occupied their bodies. Yet we see hundreds of thousands of such people become temples of the Holy Spirit.

There are only two conditions: one, repentance, and two, faith in the Lord Jesus Christ.

How? There are only two conditions: one, repentance, and two, faith in the Lord Jesus Christ.

- REPENTANCE -

Jesus said: *"'I will ask the Father, and he will give you another Counselor ..., The world cannot accept him'"* (John 14:16, 17, NIV). Peter said: *"Repent ye therefore, and be converted, that your sins may be blotted out, when times of refreshing shall come from the presence of the Lord. Repent ... for the remission of sins, and ye shall receive the gift of the Holy Ghost"* (Acts 2:38; 3:19, KJV).

The Holy Spirit is a most holy Being. The Bible uses the image of a dove for the Holy Spirit. A dove is a clean bird; it will not build its nest on a dunghill. The Holy Spirit will not settle in a sinful life; He is too sensitive. Heavenly waters do not flow through polluted channels, through neither foul minds nor foul mouths.

The Holy Spirit is only for the blood-washed sons and daughters of God. Nobody can be good enough until cleansed in Calvary's fountain. Blood comes before fire. No other cleansing is necessary or possible. We cannot make ourselves more holy or more worthy than the blood of Jesus already makes us. The Holy Spirit is a gift and cannot be earned.

We cannot make ourselves more holy or more worthy than the blood of Jesus already makes us. The Holy Spirit is a gift and cannot be earned.

- FAITH -

And without faith it is impossible to please God, because anyone who comes to him must believe that he exists and that he rewards those who earnestly seek him. (Hebrews 11:6, NIV)

By this he meant the Spirit, whom those who believed in him were later to receive. (John 7:39, NIV)

You foolish Galatians! Did you receive the Spirit by observing the law, or by believing what you heard? (Galatians 3:1-2, NIV)

To come to Jesus begging and pleading is not having faith at all. Faith involves taking.

To come to Jesus begging and pleading is not having faith at all. FAITH INVOLVES TAKING. You do not need to persuade Jesus Christ to be kind and baptize you in His holy fire. He has already promised. Come with boldness to collect what He is offering you. It is a gift, and you must believe the Giver before you reach out to receive what the Giver is giving.

What about "waiting in Jerusalem"? Jesus told the disciples to wait, but then the Holy Spirit *"had not been given, since Jesus had not yet been glorified"* (John 7:39, NIV). They had to wait for the historic moment. BUT NOW HE IS HERE. Pentecost is a fact and you can experience it personally. We have no pleading meetings, only receiving meetings. Jesus loves to fulfill His Word in our lives. We are believers, not beggars.

THE HOLY LANGUAGE

When we receive the original baptism with the Spirit, the original signs will follow.

All of them were filled with the Holy Spirit and began to speak in other tongues as the Spirit enabled them. (Acts 2:4, NIV)

How? The 120 disciples were praising the Lord. Then came the *"rush of a mighty wind"* (Acts 2:2, RSV) and the tongues of flame, and their hearts exploded with joy. They opened their mouths to speak, and the Spirit gave them utterance in languages unknown to them. Just like that.

If we receive the same baptism, it must have the same effect. Jesus the Baptizer has not changed, nor have His methods. In God's kingdom we are not copies of copies, but originals from The Original JESUS CHRIST.

If we receive the same baptism, it must have the same effect. Jesus the Baptizer has not changed, nor have His methods. In God's kingdom we are not copies of copies, but originals from The Original, JESUS CHRIST. When we experience the baptism in the Holy Spirit, we do not receive leftovers, but the original experience.

The ability to speak in tongues is mentioned throughout the book of Acts:

> *The circumcised believers who had come with Peter were astonished that the gift of the Holy Spirit had been poured out even on the Gentiles. For they heard them speaking in tongues and praising God.* (Acts 10:45-46, NIV)

Speaking in tongues was taken by the apostle Paul as evidence of the baptism in the Holy Spirit. Simon the Sorcerer "saw" the no doubt supernatural manifestation of the Spirit (Acts 8:17-19). Paul received the baptism (Acts 9:17) and said he spoke with tongues (1 Corinthians 14:18). On other occasions the same thing is reported (Acts 11:17, 13:52, 19:6).

Tongues is the only language the devil cannot understand. The archconfuser is totally confused himself, because he does not even know the alphabet of the Holy Spirit. Satan cannot crack the Holy Spirit's secret code which puts us in touch with the throne of heaven.

On the Day of Pentecost Peter explained what was happening by quoting Joel (Acts 2:17-19). Joel had prophesied that people would prophesy. When they spoke with tongues, Peter said, "*'This is that ...'*" (Acts 2:16, KJV) Speaking with tongues, when interpreted, is prophecy.

What better sign could God give to make us confident that the Holy Spirit is within and upon us as we go out to preach the Gospel? When we feel weak and fearful and hard-pressed as Paul did (1 Corinthians 2:3), the wonder of tongues assures us. Without some outward manifestation we could pray forever without being sure, and that is exactly what has happened.

What a wonderful thing! Paul described speaking in tongues as telling secrets to God (1 Corinthians 14:2). Tongues is the only language the devil cannot understand. The archconfuser is totally confused himself, because he does not even know the alphabet of the Holy Spirit. Satan cannot crack the Holy Spirit's secret code which puts us in touch with the throne of heaven.

Our bodies are *"temples of the Holy Spirit"* (1 Corinthians 6:19, NIV). Jesus said a temple was a house of prayer (Matthew 21:13, Mark 11:17). If our bodies are temples, houses of prayer in which the Spirit dwells, then He will pray through us, pure and powerful prayers, reaching the throne of God. The Spirit loves to pray, and that is why the Spirit-filled are eager to pray. It is not a sour duty but a glorious pleasure and privilege. Jesus said, *"'Howbeit when he, the Spirit of truth, is come, he ... shall glorify me'"* (John 16:13, 14, NIV).

When Solomon dedicated the Temple, the light of the "shekinah," the visible glory of God, shone on the golden Mercy Seat in the Holy of Holies. After he prayed, the entire area, the Holy Place and the outside courts, was filled with the glory so that the priests could not enter, and they fell to the floor in worship and thanksgiving (2 Chronicles 7:1-3). That is an Old Testament picture.

If we are saved, the light of Christ dwells in the shrine of our inner hearts, but when we pray for the Holy Spirit, He breaks forth throughout our entire beings, spirit, soul, mind and body. He floods and baptizes our whole personalities.

When we pray for the Holy Spirit, He breaks forth throughout our entire beings, spirit, soul, mind and body.

Finally, ask, that is all. When we are cleansed through the redeeming blood of Jesus, we are children of God. The baptism in the Holy Spirit becomes our birthright. Jesus encourages us especially about that gift: *"'Ask... seek ... knock ... For everyone who asks receives; he who seeks finds; and to him who knocks, the door will be opened'"* (Luke 11:9-10). Ask *"in faith, nothing wavering,"* as James said (James 1:6, KJV).

No foul demon can impersonate the Holy Spirit and come in His disguise.

What we receive will only be from God. The devil never answers prayers prayed in the name of Jesus. He has no means of tapping our direct line to heaven if we ask the heavenly Father for the Holy Spirit. No foul demon can impersonate the Holy Spirit and come in His disguise. Read what Jesus said:

> *"Which of you fathers, if your son asks for a fish, will give him a snake instead? Or if he asks for an egg, will give him a scorpion? If you then, though you are evil, know how to give good gifts to your children, how much more will your Father in heaven give the Holy Spirit to those who ask him!"* (Luke 11:11-13, NIV)

That is the final answer. We could not have a more explicit assurance.

WHAT YOU MUST DO NOW

Now that you have read this booklet, you know what the Lord intends to do in your life: baptize you with the Holy Spirit. Remember that JESUS, and JESUS alone, is the Baptizer (John 1:33). And He is with you right now.

If you have been washed in the blood of the Lamb of God of all your sins, then you qualify to receive this glorious gift. You need not even wait for any special church service. Jesus is with you this very moment. Begin to praise His name. **ASK NOW!** Worship the Lord, praise His name, and you will be baptized by Jesus Christ with the Holy Spirit and with fire.

If you have been washed in the blood of the Lamb of God of all your sins, then you qualify to receive this glorious gift.

What the early Christians had is as much for you as for anyone else because Jesus loves you. Remember, Jesus does not need persuading to do this. He did not need persuading to love you, and He loves you enough to baptize you with the Holy Spirit, now ... **RIGHT NOW.**

*****

Notes

Other books & booklets by Reinhard Bonnke

Faith for the Night

In this booklet Evangelist Bonnke explains that faith is like a wiring system that carries power into our lives.
Faith itself is not the power, but it links us to the power source. There is no link to God's power without faith!

- Approx 28 pages
- ISBN 3-935057-16-4

How to have Assurance of Salvation

This booklet tackles the first and most vital crisis that every new believer faces. Before anything else, we must know we are saved! It is the crucial link between salvation and discipleship. Using graphic illustrations from Scripture, this message forms the basis of the booklet Now that You are Saved, given to new believers in every CfaN campaign.

- Approx 26 pages
- ISBN 3-935057-11-3

First of all... Intercession

"Evangelism without intercession is like an explosive without a detonator," says Reinhard Bonnke. Christians have a world to reclaim and regain for God. Prayer and intercession cast out the entrenched enemy, violate his borders and retake lost territory. This booklet explains the task of intercession clearly and concisely, and encourages Christians to use the weapon of prayer more consistently and effectively.

- Approx 28 pages
- ISBN 3-935057-17-2

The Secret of the Power of the Blood of Jesus

The blood type of Jesus is unique. Since it was spiritually created it has spiritual power. As a young evangelist Reinhard Bonnke vowed that wherever he went he would preach on the blood of Jesus. This booklet contains that powerful gospel message in all its life-changing anointing.

- Approx 26 pages
- ISBN 3-935057-10-5

How to Receive a Miracle from God

Perhaps the greatest single obstacle to accepting the reality of miracles is our inability to understand God's dynamics. The dynamics of the miraculous are the Word of God, Faith and Obedience. When these three are in place, miracles happen. This booklet will unlock the doors of unbelieving hearts to expect a miracle from God.

- Approx 24 pages
- ISBN 3-935057-13-X

The Lord Your Healer

God loves to heal. He still heals today. During CfaN campaigns, we see thousands receive healing and remain totally healed. This straight forward but profound booklet answers the critics and lifts our faith. We do not look to church leaders, special ministries or Reinhard Bonnke for healing, but to Jesus. He will answer.

- Approx 24 pages
- ISBN 3-935057-14-8

Redemption... The Romance of Redeeming Love

When God gave his son Jesus to die for us, it cost him everything. The gift of Redemption is the ultimate expression of God's love. This booklet reveals through Scripture, God's unique and perfect Redemption plan. Creation was easy, but for our Redemption, God gave himself.

- Approx 30 pages
- ISBN 3-935057-15-6

Faith... the Link with God's Power

Reinhard Bonnke draws from his years of personal study and ministry to millions to reveal that Faith is the fertile ground in which God moves and that it is not the size of your faith, but the size of the God you believe in that determines the results. Faith is like a wiring system that carries power into our lives. Faith itself is not the power, but it links us to the power source. There is no link to God's power without faith.

- Approx 300 pages
- ISBN 3-935057-29-6

Mighty Manifestations

A book to challenge the believer to step out and use the "power tools of God", the gifts of the Holy Spirit. All the gifts are covered in detail. Reinhard Bonnke shows how we can be effective in using the gifts we have been given.

- Approx 226 pages
- 16 page colour photo section
- Supporting Workbook & Study Guide available
- ISBN 0-88419-386-1

Evangelism by Fire
Igniting your passion for the lost
"This book is not only mighty, but it is meaty! It will rekindle the corners of your soul and turn its centre to a white-hot focus on what matters most to God–the salvation and deliverance of eternal souls. Bonnke's words have a way of bringing you to that alter anew–to be baptised with Jesus' fire once again."
Jack W. Hayford, D. Litt.

- Approx 320 pages
- 16 page colour photo section
- Supporting Workbook & Study Guide available
- ISBN 3-935057-19-9

For further information about these and other products, please contact your nearest outlet:

Full Flame, GmbH
Postfach 60 05 95
60335 Frankfurt am Main
Germany

www.fullflame.com
info@fullflame.com

Full Flame, LLC
P.O. Box 593647
Orlando, FL 32859
USA

www.fullflameonline.com
info@fullflameonline.com

For further details of the CfaN ministry please contact the office nearest to you:

Christ for all Nations
Postfach 60 05 74
60335 Frankfurt am Main
Germany

Internet: www.cfan.org

Christ for all Nations
P.O. 590588
Orlando
FL 32859-0588, USA

E-mail: info@cfan.org